What's it Like?

Blindness

Angela Royston

Heinemann
LIBRARY

Young Explorer

H **www.heinemann.co.uk/library**
Visit our website to find out more information about **Heinemann Library** books.

To order:
☎ Phone 44 (0) 1865 888066
▤ Send a fax to 44 (0) 1865 314091
💻 Visit the Heinemann Bookshop at www.heinemann.co.uk/library to browse our catalogue and order online.

First published in Great Britain by Heinemann Library, Halley Court, Jordan Hill, Oxford OX2 8EJ, part of Harcourt Education.
Heinemann is a registered trademark of Harcourt Education Ltd.

Editorial: Sarah Shannon and Richard Woodham
Design: Ron Kamen, Victoria Bevan and Celia Jones
Picture Research: Maria Joannou and Kay Altwegg
Production: Amanda Meaden

Originated by Dot Gradations Ltd
Printed and bound in China by South China Printing Company

ISBN 0 431 11223 1
09 08 07 06 05
10 9 8 7 6 5 4 3 2 1

British Library Cataloguing in Publication Data
Royston, Angela
Blindness – (What's it like?)
362.4'1

A full catalogue record for this book is available from the British Library.

Acknowledgements
The publishers would like to thank the following for permission to reproduce photographs:

Alamy pp.10 (Photofusion Picture Library), 24 (Angela Jordan), 28 (Seb Rogers); Corbis pp.13 (Ed Kashi), 21, 22 (Joe Bator); PA Photos p.20 (Kim Myung Jung Kim); Photodisc pp.11, 16; Rex Features pp.15, 23 (Tony Kyriacou), 25; Science Photo Library pp.4 (Martin Riedl), 6, 7, 8 (Sue Ford), 9 (Steve Allen), 12 (P.Dury/Publiphoto Diffusion); Topham Picturepoint p.19 (ImageWorks); Tudor Photography pp.5, 17, 18, 26, 27, 29; Zefa p.14.

Cover photograph of a blind boy with a pop-up book reproduced with permission of the RNIB.

Every effort has been made to contact copyright holders of any material reproduced in this book. Any omissions will be rectified in subsequent printings if notice is given to the publishers.

The publishers would like to thank the Oxfordshire Association for the Blind for their help in the preparation of this book.

The paper used to print this book comes from sustainable resources.

Contents

Words appearing in the text in bold, **like this**, are explained in the Glossary.

 Find out more about what it's like to be blind at www.heinemannexplore.co.uk

What is blindness?

You see with your eyes. Many people's eyes do not work as well as they should. Most of these people wear glasses to help them see more clearly.

Some people cannot see well even with glasses. If a person can only see a little, they are **partially sighted**. A blind person can see nothing or almost nothing.

You cannot always tell if someone is blind.

How you see

You see when light bounces off an object and into your eyes. The light goes into your eye through a dark circle in the centre called the **pupil**.

We are able to see a spider's web because of the light that bounces off it.

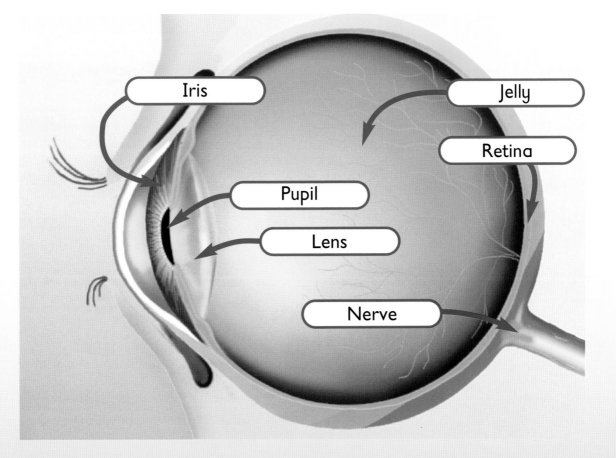

Light passes through the **lens** of your eye and makes a clear picture on the **retina**. A **nerve** sends the picture from the retina to your **brain**.

Causes of blindness

There are many different causes of blindness. A **cataract** makes the **lens** of the eye go cloudy. Some diseases can affect the jelly inside the eyeball.

Cataracts make it hard to see clearly.

This is a close-up of a retina.

Most diseases that cause blindness affect the **retina**. Doctors do not know what causes many of these diseases. You cannot catch blindness from someone who is blind.

Who is blind?

People of all ages can be blind, but most people with poor eyesight are older people. Many of the diseases that cause blindness affect older people more than younger people.

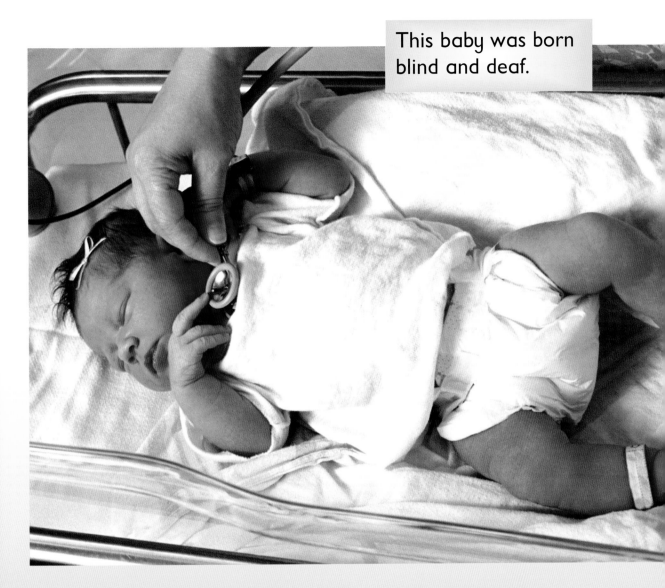

This baby was born blind and deaf.

Some people are born blind, especially babies that are born too early. Other people become blind because of an accident that damages their eyes.

11

Helping blindness

A **partially sighted** person can use a **magnifying glass** to see more clearly. The magnifying glass makes reading easier by making the words look bigger.

A magnifying glass can help a partially sighted person to read more easily.

This person is being tested for cataracts.

Some kinds of blindness can be cured with an **operation**. If someone has a **cataract**, an eye **surgeon** can remove the cloudy **lens** and put in a small plastic lens instead.

Living with blindness

People who are blind can do most things that sighted people can. Instead of looking with their eyes, they feel and smell things, and listen out for sounds.

A blind person uses the senses of touch and smell to prepare a meal.

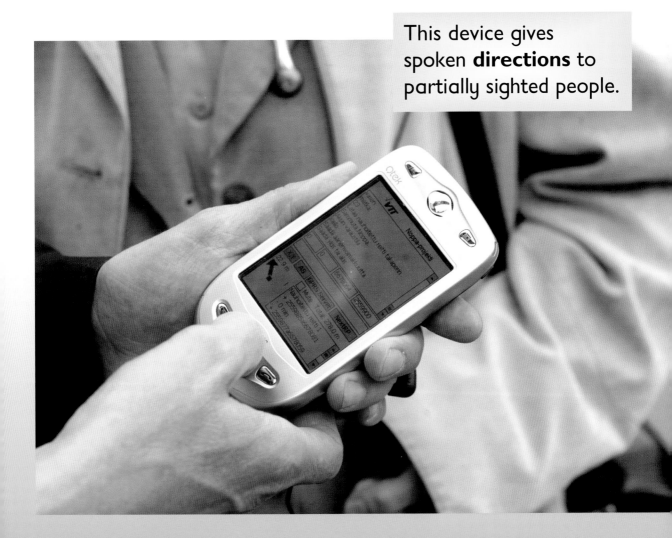

Blind people may sometimes need help, but they usually like to do things themselves. It is easier for them if everything is always stored in the same place.

Going out

Many blind people use a white stick when they go outside. They use it to feel the ground ahead for lamp posts, steps, and other **obstacles**.

A white stick also warns people that a person is blind.

Blind people listen out for footsteps and other noises. For example, many lift doors bleep when they are about to close.

The smell of bread helps this person recognize where she is.

Guide dogs

Specially trained guide dogs can help blind people find their way outside. A guide dog is trained to help a blind person avoid **obstacles**.

Having a guide dog gives a blind person more freedom.

A guide dog is always looking out for obstacles.

If you meet a person with a guide dog, do not stroke or talk to the dog. Leave the dog alone so it can get on with its work.

Crossing the road

Many pavements are built to be helpful to blind people. In some places the pavement may be bumpy instead of flat. The bumps help a blind person feel where there is a **pedestrian crossing**.

These bumps can be felt by a blind person walking past.

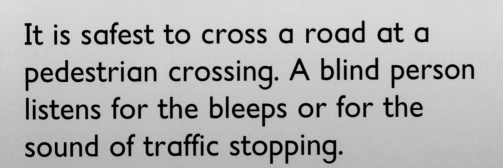

The bleeps made by a pedestrian crossing tell a blind person when it is safe to cross the road.

It is safest to cross a road at a pedestrian crossing. A blind person listens for the bleeps or for the sound of traffic stopping.

Reading

Blind people can read books. **Braille** is a code that changes letters into a pattern of raised dots. The person feels the dots to read the words.

Talking books are a good way for blind people to enjoy books.

A talking book is a recording of an actor reading a book out loud. Talking books come on cassettes or **CDs**. Everyone can enjoy a talking book!

Gardens and museums

Some gardens are specially planted for blind people to enjoy. Many of the plants have strong smells. Others have leaves that are interesting to feel.

This garden has been made for blind people to enjoy. The flowers produce many different smells.

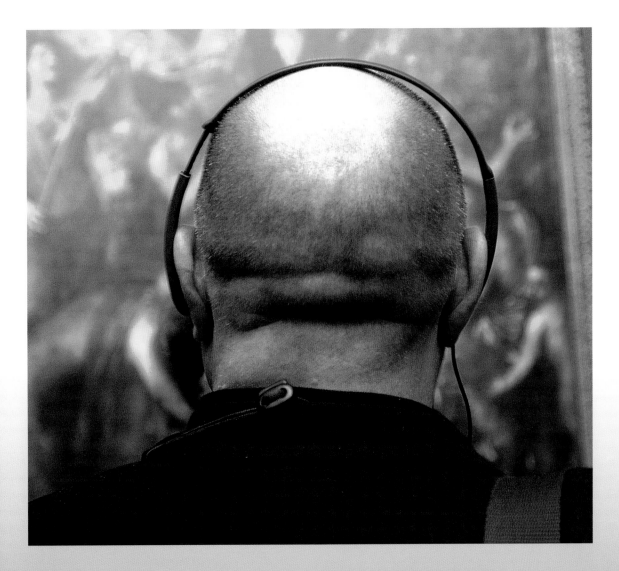

Most **museums** and **art galleries** have **audio guides** for blind people to use. The person can listen to a voice that describes the objects or paintings.

Working

Blind people do many kinds of jobs. A blind person can become a train driver or a **television presenter** for example.

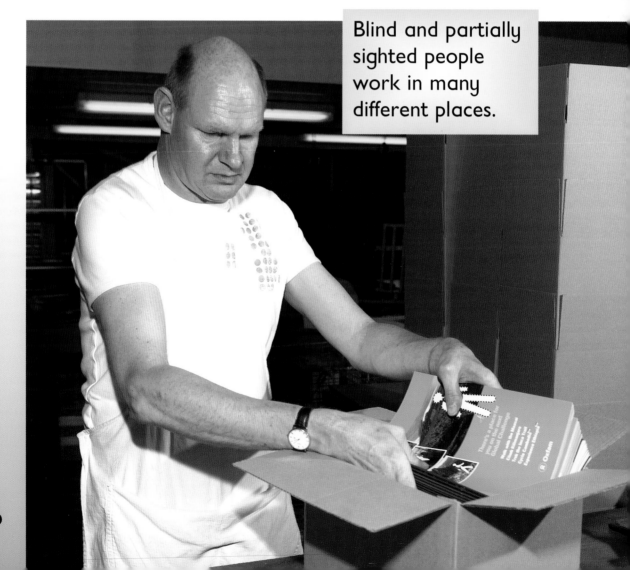

Blind and partially sighted people work in many different places.

Blind people can use computers. People with no sight can use software that speaks the words. People who are **partially sighted** can make the words larger on the computer screen.

Enjoying life

Many blind people enjoy playing sport. Some play cricket with a special ball that makes a noise. Players hear the ball rather than see it.

A blind person rides behind a sighted person on a **tandem**.

Blind people swim and take part in
sports such as bowls, football, and golf.
In golf, a helper guides the blind person
around the course.

Find out more

British Blind Sport
Read about how you can get involved in sports for the blind and **partially sighted**.
www.britishblindsport.org.uk

The Guide Dogs for the Blind Association
Learn about how guide dogs are trained, and how they have changed the lives of blind people.
www.guidedogs.org.uk

Healthy Eyes
Click on 'kids' to find out more about how you see.
www.healthyeyes.org.uk

 Find out more about what it's like to be blind at www.heinemannexplore.co.uk

Disclaimer
All the internet addresses (URLs) given in this book were valid at the time of going to press. However, due to the dynamic nature of the Internet, some addresses may have changed, or sites may have ceased to exist since publication. While the author and publishers regret any inconvenience this may cause readers, no responsibility for any such changes can be accepted by either the author or the publishers.

Glossary

art gallery place where paintings and other art are on display

audio guide spoken description of something that people listen to in, for example, a museum

Braille way of writing using patterns of raised dots instead of letters and numerals. A person reads by feeling the dots with their hands.

brain part of the body that controls the rest of your body and with which you think

cataract eye disease that makes the lens in the eye go cloudy

CD compact disc

directions instructions that tell how how to get to places

iris coloured part of the eye, surrounding the pupil

lens part of the eye that collects light and bends it on to the retina

magnifying glass large curved glass that makes things look bigger

museum place where rare, valuable, and interesting things are kept and shown to the public

nerve part of the body that carries messages to and from the brain

obstacle something that is in the way

operation when a surgeon works on a part of the body to repair it

partially sighted able to see a little, but not clearly

pedestrian crossing place where traffic should stop to let people walk across the road safely

pupil small, round hole in the coloured part of the eye

retina part of the eye that changes light into signals that go to the brain

surgeon person who performs operations

tandem bicycle that two people can ride together

television presenter person who tells you what is happening during a television or radio programme

---

More books to read

O'Neill, Linda, *Imagine: Being Blind* (Rourke Publishing, 2001)

McGinty, Alice, *Guide Dogs: Seeing for People Who Can't* (Powerkids Press, 2003)

Index